Inspirations
from the
Heart

Joanne Concepcion Sanchez

Copyright © 2021 Joanne Concepcion Sanchez
All rights reserved
First Edition

PAGE PUBLISHING, INC.
Conneaut Lake, PA

First originally published by Page Publishing 2021

Cover Art Illustrated By Millie Geibel

ISBN 978-1-6624-4512-5 (pbk)
ISBN 978-1-6624-4511-8 (digital)

Printed in the United States of America

4-9-23

Happy Easter Cathy,
May the verses in this book be of inspiration.
God bless you,
Joanne Sánchez

Dedicated to the memory of my grandmother Maria Remedio Rosario, aka Mapita. She sacrificed a lot for me, in giving me a good education, lots of love, understanding, and compassion during my childhood years. Mapita taught me to be strong, kind, and to never give up in life. It's because of all her support that I have become the woman that I am today, and I thank her with all my heart.

Contents

Sentiments 9

Family 11
Siblings 13
Luis, Louie, My Brother 14
Margarita, My Sister 15
Carmen, My Sister 16
Antonio (Tony), aka Cootie, My Brother 17
Millie (Milagros), My Sister 18
Francisco, Frankie, My Brother 19
Gilberto, My Older Brother 20

Friends 21
Friendship 23
Friend 24
Three Special Friends 25
A New Friendship 26
Airborne 27
Spiritual Friends 28
Amanda 29
Ayako 30
Emily 31
Erlinda 32
Isabelle 33
Lucila 34

Birthdays 35
Happy Birthday 37
Birthday—Far Away 38

Sweet Sixteen—Ainsley 39
Birthday—Jack..40
Sixty-fifth Birthday—Father John Grace 41
Sixty-eighth Birthday—Father Kevin..42

Nature 43
Little Sparrow...45
Spring 46
Rainfall from the Sky 47
The Rain That Falls from Heaven 48

Special Occasions..49
Wedding Congratulations (Steve and Millie) 51
A New Life—Clare and David 52
Silver Anniversary..53
Amado and Paula's Fortieth Wedding Anniversary..................54
Ed and Joyce's Golden Anniversary...55
Ordination Anniversary...56
Father Charles J. Kennedy's Tenth Ordination Anniversary 57
Father John Grace's Fiftieth Ordination Anniversary 58

Love and Romance...59
Valentine Poem 61
My Special Star...62
I Love You More...63
A Special Person 64
Boyish Smile 65
Secret Love 66
The Day You Left...67
An Emptiness..68
A Very Rainy Day..69
What Do You Do?..70
Leon Jay 71

Religion and Faith 73
Augustinian Priests 75
Kevin McManus...76

Blessed Trinity 77
Jesus Christ, Our King 78
My Heart 79
Guardian Angel 80
Inner Search 81
Shameful Ways 82
Voice of the Soul 83
Lenten Time 84
At Times (A Reflection) 85
Teacher Barbara—Bible Study 86
RCIA Team 87

Caring Physicians and Surgeons 89
Anatol Podolsky, MD 91
Joseph Mule, MD 92
Grace Young, MD 93

Precious Little Children 95
Our Precious Child 97
Danisito 98
Gabriel 99
Michelle 100
Karyna 101
Zachary 102

Christmas and New Year 103
Christmas 105
Christ's Special Birth 106
Christmas King 107
A Christmas Prayer 108
Christmas Tears 109
New Year 110

Famous People 111
Ellen Degeneres 113
Oprah 114

Painter of Light 115
William W. Clinton—President 116

Miscellaneous 117
America the Beautiful..119
"Baby" (Millie's Kitten) 120
Broken Dreams 121
Color My World..122
Forgotten Souls 123
Sadness..124
Graduation Day 125
Margaret's Meat Loaf..126
God Will Pave the Way 127
Young Ladies Institute (YLI) 128

In Memoriam..129
In Loving Memory of Justina 131
In Loving Memory of Stephanie................................132
Farewell to Velma 133
A Tribute to Mapita (My Grandmother) 134
A Tribute to Milagros (My Mother)..........................135
A Tribute to DiAngelo James Bono 136
A Tribute to Jack Lore 137
A Tribute to Salvador..138
Deceased Children 139

Sentiments

Through my poetry, I wish to express my God-given talent,
And to touch the hearts of all who read these verses.

Family

Siblings

Seven children all in all
Raised in a project when we were small
Poverty was our middle name
We didn't have much
But we loved each other just the same

Our mother did the best she could
In raising us as a mother would
Though there were times when things were rough
We all hung in there 'cause we were tough

Now we are five instead of seven
For two of us have gone to heaven
The years that passed were happy ones
For we were together and that was fun

Reflecting back on all those years
With thoughts of happy times and tears
It seemed as though time passed us by
And it's on our memories that we rely

We're siblings gone in separate ways
Yet in our hearts our love still stays
Now that we are older we can see
That the future seemed to set us free

Luis, Louie, My Brother

Lovingly, I think of you, the first one of my brothers
One Easter Sunday you were born, that day was like no other
Until you came, I was alone for seven lonely years
In just one day, my life was changed, God sent me someone dear
Even though we're seven years apart, we are very close, you see
Louie and I share a bond of love, and he means the world to me

Margarita, My Sister

Many years ago, a child was born
    with skin as white as snow
A smile that captured many hearts
    your face had such a glow
Recalling as I watched you grow
    Into a lovely teenage girl
Great was to have you in our clan
    You were as precious as a pearl
And from a teenage girl, you grew
    Into a woman oh so brave
Right then, you were amazing
    An example of strength, you gave
In other words, I'm glad you're here
    An asset to behold
Time changes many things in life
    But not a heart of gold
A mother of two you then became
    Your children were your greatest joy
Margarita, you had Stacey, a little girl
    and Frankie, a bouncing baby boy

Carmen, My Sister

Carmen, you're so special in your very loving way
Always there to lend a hand each and every day
Remembering you as a child, so lovely and so sweet
Mother of an only child has made your life complete
Endlessly, you try to please in giving all your love
Now and forever, you'll be blessed by our loving God above

Antonio (Tony), aka Cootie, My Brother

A loving soul was Tony, a brother so kind and dear
Nothing seemed to make him happy, his life was full of fear
To him, each day was meaningless, no future did he see
Oh, if he only knew his worth, how much he means to me
Now the Lord has called you home, you finally found your peace
Instead of weeping tears of sadness, you are sharing in God's feast
Only you alone have known, the rejection life can bring
Antonio, enjoy eternity and the songs the angels sing

Millie (Milagros), My Sister

Millie you are precious, a beauty to behold
In life, you've been so caring, a child as pure as gold
Letting go of all the traumas that have existed as you grew
Learning to love yourself gave you strength each day anew
I know that God has blessed you in your kind and loving ways
Everyone that you encounter, they bring sunshine to your days
Millie, you know I love you and wish you all the best
Little sister, as I pray for you, I ask your life be blest.

Francisco, Frankie, My Brother

From the time you were a baby, you were a precious little boy
Running all around the house, you brought us lots of joy
As the months and years went by, we grew to love you more
Now that you have gone to God, it's not like it was before
Knowing our little brother was a part of our Lord's plan
In green pastures, now he walks in the new and promised land
Every time we think of you, we miss you more each day
Frankie, may you rest in peace, and may God light your way

Gilberto, My Older Brother
Born in Puerto Rico

Growing up without you separated by the Caribbean sea
I didn't know you existed, yet adulthood set us free
Lovingly you made it known that we were products of our dad
Brother, many years went by now your existence made me glad
Each passing year, as we grew up in different worlds apart
Recalling you wanted a sibling for loneliness filled your heart
Together we just grew in love from the day we found each other
Oh, surely we were meant to meet though we both have different mothers

Friends

Friendship

Friendship is a gift from God
Bestowed from up above
We should cherish all the friends we have
And give them lots of love
As I reminisce down memory lane
And think of all the passing years
I recall all the friends I've had who are so very dear
Their friendship has meant the world to me
And the special times we've shared
We all have been there for each other
Because we've truly cared
I think of all the happy times
And also sad times too
Without my friends to share my life
I would have been so blue
My friends are like my family
A treasure for all time
I thank the Lord for this great gift
To me, he's been so kind
So I dedicate this poem
To all my loyal friends
God bless you for your friendship
Which we'll share until the end

Friend

He is only five feet tall
So filled with wit and charm
My friend is very loving
With a heart that's oh so warm
Whenever I am with him
He brightens up my day
I pray that he will always care for me
In his own special way
My friend, he is from Ireland, way across the sea
And I from Puerto Rico, two lands apart, you see
Yet friendship sees no boundaries
Whenever two hearts meet
For we share a common bond of love
Which is God's own special treat
So today I honor you, my friend
With all the love inside my heart
For land nor any boundaries
Will ever make our friendship part

Three Special Friends

As I walk down memory lane
And I think about my growing years
I recollect the friends I've had that are so very dear
The little Asian girl I know, **Tina** is her name
She is always filled with laughter
As we shared our many games
And **Pat** from Honolulu, always there to understand
Whenever I had many doubts,
she would take me by the hand
Then there is **Blanche**, my faithful friend
whom I will not forget
For she often showed in many ways
That she was glad we met
Now that the years have passed me by
And I reminisce again
I realize I have a treasure
In my three and special friends
I'll cherish them within my heart
Where they will always be
For **Tina**, **Pat**, and **Blanche** have endeared
themselves to me

A New Friendship

I've met a friend from a foreign land
Where the grass is emerald green
She has come to America from Ireland
Fulfilling a vacationing dream
From that first meeting, we knew right then
That our friendship was meant to be
And although we are different in many ways
The Lord helped us to see
Friendships are made from the heart and caring
It's a special gift bestowed from above
Like a flower, it grows and it grows
When sprinkled with lots of love
So may God bless our friendship
Even though you're far away
I'll remember our first special meeting
My friend, I'll pray for you each day

Airborne

Flying in the sky so high
A new friendship was created
We spoke and shared
Our regrets and dreams
All of which seemed overrated
We had some things in common
And in a short time the friendship grew
Then it was time to disembark the plane
The one in which we flew
We parted as we said goodbye
Until we meet again
It goes to show you that you never
Know where you will meet a friend

Spiritual Friends

My dear friends at **St. Pius V**, we gather to join in prayer
Our spiritual director starts with songs for us to share
Relying on the grace of God, we laugh, we joke, we sing
Each of us so happy with just what our friendship brings
We always praise the Lord with joy in all the things we do
We are a family of our God, and that's so very true

Amanda

An Indonesian girl who came from far away
Miles separated her from home, now in the USA
Always cheerful in her ways, as pleasant as can be
Now she's found many friends in people just like me
Doing all to please the Lord, she does it with such zest
Amanda, you are special, God knows you do your best

Ayako

A lot of times we take for granted the things we cherish most
Years of a growing friendship like the one that brought us close
And now as you celebrate your ***seventieth***, I want to wish you all the best
Knowing you throughout the years, I feel my life's been blest
Oh, how I am so fortunate to have a ***best friend*** real and true
Ayako, you're special to me, and with the years our friendship grew

Emily

Emily, you are so special in all the things you do
May the Lord and angels bless you for your faith in God is true
In all that you've accomplished throughout the many years
Lovingly you've done it all with sweat as well as tears
You've earned your golden crown of jewels in heaven high above
Emily, God sees your faithful heart that's full of so much love

Erlinda

Erlinda is my special friend, one whom I cherish most
Recalling how she loves our Lord has brought us very close
Lovingly, she's touched the hearts of her family oh so dear
In every aspect of her life, her love has been made clear
Now today you're turning **seventy**, and I wish you all the best
Doctor Linda, knowing you for years, I feel my life's been blest
As time goes by, may our friendship grow, and may it last forever
Erlinda, the bond that we both share is what brought us close together

Isabelle

In many ways, you're gifted with great faith in God above
Sharing your love with the kindness we are all deserving of
As always, you pray for those who mean the world to you
Bravely confronting life's ups and downs, to God remaining true
Even when the going was tough, you held your head up high
Living each day to the fullest and never asking why
Lovingly, you touched the lives of your children oh so dear
Every flower in your garden, you planted with such cheer
Isabelle, this tribute has been written especially for you
A friend who thinks you're special who really means it too

Lucila

L is for the laughter you've brought with all your jokes
U is the unending smiles you've shared with many folks
C is for your caring ways that are a part of you
I is for the interest shown, which seems to be so true
L is for the long years that you've served at Schuelke North
A is the announcement of your birthday, **fifty** years, of course
So what does the above spell out? *Lucila* is the name
A girl whose been around a lot and knows that life's a game

Birthdays

Happy Birthday

Wishing you a birthday
that is special just like you
A birthday that is joyous
in all the things you do
A birthday that reminds you of
cherished memories in the past
A birthday filled with lots of love
and hugs that will always last
So on your special day
I wish you lots of laughter
Not only on this birthday
But for now and ever after

Birthday—Far Away

Happy birthday, precious angel
May your wishes all come true
My prayers are for your happiness
That your days are seldom blue
I'm also sending all my love
From deep within my heart
I wish I could be there with you
But through fate we had to part
Although you're far away from me
My love for you still grows
You're my special gift from God
I adore you and it shows
So have a Happy birthday
May your life be filled with love
I bless the day I met you
And I thank the Lord above

Sweet Sixteen—Ainsley

A special girl named Ainsley has turned sixteen today
In all her growing years, she's been loved in many ways
Now as I write this tribute to express just how I feel
Surely, words are not enough, for your heart Ainsley will steal
Lucky is our family, and with pride we give our love
Even though you're just sixteen, you're a blessing from above
You're so mature beyond your years, a beauty to behold
Ainsley, never change your ways, for you have a heart of gold

Birthday — Jack

Just a wish for happiness on your special day
Another birthday here again, how time sure fades away
Caring with your cheerful smile keeps you so young at heart
Knowing you and liking you is what sets you apart
So who's the person who I honor on this very special day?
It's ***Jack,*** my friend, of course, and may God just light his way

Sixty-fifth Birthday— Father John Grace

Happy birthday, Father Grace, today you're sixty-five
Another milestone you have reached, another year survived
You've helped so many people and accomplished many things
You deserve to have a happy day, and the best that life can bring
The silver highlights in your hair reflect the wisdom you have gained
Each stepping stone throughout your life has won you lots of fame
So know that special friendships can never be replaced
God bless you and best wishes, my dear friend, Father John Grace

Sixty-eighth Birthday— Father Kevin

Happy birthday, special friend, be happy on this day
I send you lots of hugs even though you're far away
I'd like to celebrate with you, but since it cannot be
I'm glad the Lord created you to be a friend to me
I'm wishing you a birthday that is special just like you
A day that will be joyous in everything you do
So, Father Kevin, on this day I wish you joy and laughter
May many blessings come your way for now and ever after

Nature

Little Sparrow

Little sparrow on a tree
Chirping your song so heavenly
What a lovely tune you sing
A gift from God is what you bring

You're oh so cheerful as you fly
When spring is here and winter dies
You sing your melody anew
Little sparrow, I love you

Little sparrow, chirp away
I love to hear your song each day
Your little beak rings out with glee
It brings me joy, please sing to me

Spring

Spring awakens all the senses
As we watch the world turn green
Spring, a time of rejuvenation
A time to plan our future dreams

Spring is when the bluebirds sing
A love song for all to hear
What a beautiful time this season
When we know that spring is near

Spring is when the heart rejoices
When couples seem to fall in love
In spring, the stars they shine so brightly
The moonbeams sparkle from above

Spring, a time for reminiscing
Of all the winters that have passed
It's to view the new horizons
Of new beginnings that will last

Rainfall from the Sky

As I watch the rain fall from the sky
I think of how the heavens cry
They're tears shed from our Savior's eyes
For the sins that cause people to die

As I watch the rain fall from the sky
I also think of days gone by
When I first learned the gift of prayer
And how I knew God really cared

As I watch the rain fall from the sky
I now know sunshine will arise
That sunny days will dry the tears
And the raindrops will finally disappear

The Rain That Falls from Heaven

The rain that falls from heaven are tears upon the earth
We all have many ups and downs from the moment of our birth

The rain that falls from heaven does a cleansing of the soul
As we struggle with life's problems just to reach our lifelong goals

The rain that falls from heaven cannot melt away the pain
Yet when we try to ease our burdens, sometimes nothing can be gained

The rain that falls from heaven cannot wash away our tears
As long as we are on this earth, we will struggle through the years

Special Occasions

Wedding Congratulations
(Steve and Millie)

So many years you've been together, and your wedding day is here
Today becoming man and wife, your vows are stated clear
Each word you say comes from your heart, to love and to obey
Visions of your life together bring much happiness your way
Every step, each moment that you share, will challenge you in life
Steve, I know you're proud today as you take Millie for your wife

May the Lord bring blessings to you both in everything you do
I know you will walk hand in hand whenever skies are blue
Love seems to conquer many things, many challenges you'll face
Look to new horizons in each day, God will shower you with grace
In taking your loving vows today, you've pledged eternal love
Everything your hearts will share will be blessed from up above

A New Life—Clare and David

Congratulations, Clare, as you start in your brand-new life
Love again has touched your heart now that you're David's wife
Always so cheerful and so kind, we will miss your loving ways
Remembering the good times had by all on very special days
Everything you are today is God's great gift to you
You brighten up the lives of others in all the things you do

David chose you to be his wife, and you make his life complete
An answer to his prayers came true with a girl who's oh so sweet
Very little did you know that your hearts would beat as one
In just a short time, you've been blest, now your future has begun
David and Clare, two special friends whom I recall with lots of love
Your friendship has been a gift to me bestowed from God above

Silver Anniversary

Many years have come and gone, your twenty-fifth is here
Another anniversary, another joyous year
Recalling your first meeting with the one to share your life
Guessing only that your girl would surely be your wife
Accepting all the good and bad as both your lives entwined
Reaching to each other, you knew all would be just fine
Everlasting is your love and the life that you have shared
Together you would conquer all, and why, because you've cared
At first, you didn't realize how much your love would grow
Right then and from the very start, love from your hearts did flow
Now twenty-five years have passed, and she's still your lady sweet
You're her prince in shining armor and her very special treat
Learning from each other throughout the years, a challenge in itself
You both have won the jackpot for your children are your wealth
And so on this silver anniversary, I wish you all the best
But most of all, I pray to God that both your lives be blest

Amado and Paula's Fortieth Wedding Anniversary

An anniversary celebration, another joyous year
Many seasons have come and gone, now your fortieth is here
Accepting all the ups and downs as both your lives entwined
Doing what your hearts dictated, you knew all would be just fine
Oh, how your love has fully grown throughout the passing years
Amado took *Paula* as his wife with a heart that was sincere

Proudly, you walked down the aisle and made your dreams come true
Always believing the best in each other, facing the struggles life threw
Until that special day you met, your lives seemed incomplete
Love came and captured both your hearts, destiny meant for you to meet
And now you leave to start a new life in Georgia, a state so far away
Paula and *Amado,* I wish you the best, may God bless you both each day

Ed and Joyce's Golden Anniversary

Each year you are together, your love just grows and grows
Destiny was in your corner, in your relationship it shows
Joys and tears you both have shared throughout your life together
Over fifty years of marriage, there was nothing you couldn't weather
Yet you are an inspiration to those who hold you dear
Committed to the vows you took which reflect your fifty years
Every day has made you wiser in your love and in your life
Ed, you were a very happy man the day you made ***Joyce*** your wife

Ordination Anniversary

It's your ordination anniversary, and the Lord smiles down on you
He knows how faithful you have been to your priestly vows so true
You've sacrificed your life for him in tending to his flock
You responded yes within your heart on the very day he knocked
So as you continue serving God with kindness and much love
Wherever life may lead you, you'll be blessed by the Lord above

Father Charles J. Kennedy's Tenth Ordination Anniversary

It's your ten-year anniversary
at St. Aloysius Church
Father Kennedy, when you came to us
It ended all our search
The first time that we met you
You made us feel at ease
Showing an interest in our people
And in all ways trying to please
Your devotion and your love
You have shared throughout the years
In your actions and your caring
You have wiped away our tears
Everything you do with pride
And so lovingly from the heart
Knowing you has gladdened all of us
Right from the very start
You have served the Hispanic people
With such passion and such love
That the Lord looks down with pride at you
As he gazes from above
So we wish you congratulations,
Happiness, and all life's best
We are proud to have you as our priest
And your prayers are our request

Father John Grace's Fiftieth Ordination Anniversary

You've given fifty years of service to Jesus Christ the King
In all your faithful ministries, loyalty and love you bring
You've served the Lord unselfishly throughout the many years
He knows you're very special, and all your prayers he hears
Your priesthood has taken you to many foreign lands
You've fulfilled for love of God the things that he has planned
On this golden anniversary, congratulations are expressed
Father John, in your fidelity, you have given God your very best

Love and Romance

Valentine Poem

Roses are a gift of love, violets can be too
Yet the greatest gift that I can give
Is my whole heart fully to you

Take it with all my love
And always keep in mind
I will love you for always
Until the end of time

Never doubt the way I feel
Because my love is true
So, darling, take your hand in mine
So we will not be blue

For you are the love of my life
And I knew it from the start
That is why I've given you my love
As well as all my heart

My Special Star

As I gaze up at the heavens and see my special star
I often wish the very best will come to you and I
May we receive the love that now our hearts do share
These loving feelings deep within express a love so rare
My special star shines brightly and releases rays of love
And let us tell it all our dreams that we're so deserving of
Now I give to you my special star so make it your star too
For when you gaze upon it, you will feel my love so true
My heart is yours forever, that's what I tell my lovely star
You are my special someone when you're near or very far

I Love You More

I love you more than words can say
More than the ocean wide
I love you more than the raindrops
That fill a stormy sky

I love you more than teardrops
That come with joy and pain
More than the leaves upon a tree
Or drops from an autumn's rain

So how much do I love you?
The question seems to ring
I love you more than life itself
Much more than anything

A Special Person

From the first day that I met you
I knew you'd have my heart
You were my precious treasure
Right from the very start
The more I got to know you
The greater my love grew
I thank the Lord for sending me
A special person, you

I treasure every moment
Whenever you are near
I know exactly how I feel
My heart has made it clear
I will love you for always
No matter where you are
You're in my heart and in my soul
Whether you are near or far

I cherish you, your smiles, your ways
And all the things you do
My world is filled with happiness
Whenever I'm with you
So, darling, please remember that
No one could love you more than I
You are my everything, dear love
The universe, the stars, and sky

Boyish Smile

When I look at your handsome face and see that boyish smile
I want to hold you in my arms for longer than awhile
My heart just seems to melt whenever you are near
I can't deny I love you, and that is what I fear

I wish that I could let you know exactly how I feel
But that would only break my heart for I know it can't be real
Good friends are all that we could be until the end of time
There is no way in this life that you could ever be mine

So continue with your boyish smile for that's all that we can share
It's hard to love someone so much and hard to truly care
Since friends is all that we can be for lovers would be wrong
I'm grateful for your friendship, although my love is strong

My feelings will not interfere with a friendship that's so secure
For loving you in other ways would be wrong, that's for sure
God bless you, precious darling, I love you with all my heart
For loving you was easy right from the very start

Secret Love

Although I've known you for so long
You are my secret love
You're like an angel from the sky
Just sent from up above
I didn't know that I could love
Or feel this way again
You've opened up my empty heart
And once again I win

Your look just magnifies my soul
You are my one desire
But it's not meant for us to be
Because we both belong to others
You'll always be my secret love
And dwell within my heart
Remember that my love endures
Like from the very start

You've become my inspiration
A dream that cannot be
But where there's life, there's also hope
And someday, we'll be set free
And then our hearts will be as one
We'll share a life together
I love you, secret love of mine
For now and then forever

The Day You Left

The day you left and went away
My world just fell apart
My tears were just like crystals
Poured from a broken heart
I love you with all my being
And thought this pain would end
But as the years fly by, my love
I just cannot pretend
I try to smile at passersby
My sadness I cannot hide
My fragile heart is broken
From so much pain inside
I miss you oh so very much
And I know I must let go
But you dwell always in my heart
And my love just seems to grow
At times, I am so lonely
And feel you've forgotten me
I guess deep down inside I knew
Our love could never be
So be happy, precious angel
My love will never die
I miss you oh so very much
And that's why each day I cry

An Emptiness

Why do I feel such emptiness?
Whenever we're apart
I miss you oh so very much
Causing pain within my heart
I wish that you would feel the same
And let me read your mind
But letting your defenses down
To you would be a crime

You'll never know the love I feel
Whenever you are near
Or the empty void left in my heart
When you're gone is what I fear
So try to understand, my love
That I need you by my side
To love you and to cherish you
To even be your guide

So let down your defenses
And let my love come in
Share my life, my hopes, my dreams
And together we both win
Don't turn away from me again
The way that you have done
We need each other, love of mine
For one day we'll be as one

A Very Rainy Day

As I look out to the heavens
On this wet and rainy day
I think of you, my love
And the fact you're far away

I visualize your gorgeous smile
Your precious eyes of blue
And in my heart, you're here with me
Love of my life, it's true

For death cannot keep us apart
You're my one and own true love
Forever you are in my heart
You were my gift from God above

So always remember, my darling
Whether you're far away or near
I am yours for all eternity
I just want to make that clear

What Do You Do?

In life, we want what we cannot have or what is already taken
So what do you do with deep feelings in your heart?
Do they all have to be forsaken?
What do you do when your mind says no?
Yet your heart is so full of love
Do you watch from a distance and fantasize
That he's the one sent to you from above?
What do you do when you know how you feel?
But with him you don't know where you stand
Do you make believe that he cares for you
As you visualize you both hand in hand?
So what do you do when you know in your heart
That you are dreaming an impossible dream?
You just cherish each moment that you spend with him
Even though things may not be what they seem
So what do you do when the person you love
Is so far, very far, from your reach?
Be grateful to know him, love him, respect him
Which is a great lesson to teach

Leon Jay

L is for the love I feel for you deep within my heart
Everlasting is your gift that's been there from the start
Only you and you alone can fill my life with laughter
No one will ever take your place for now or ever after
Joyous was the day we met, a coincidence, it's true
As I look back and reminisce, your leaving made me blue
Yet life may just be borrowed, but one's love never dies,
Leon Jay, although I miss you, my eyes no longer cry

Religion and Faith

Augustinian Priests

As I sit here reminiscing of the many years we've shared
I think of all the Augustinian priests and just how much they cared

Fr. Kevin, who's our pastor, likes to play guitar and sing
Every Friday night we'd join him, singing praises to our King

Then there's **Fr. Grace** in Alpha, our spiritual leader as he'd speak
We got closer to our Savior and to each other every week

We're at a dance, it's St. Patrick's Day, **Fr. Brennan** is our guest
He entertains us with a Gaelic song, he performs his very best

A deep voice rings out at St. Pius V, with a message loud and clear
It's **Fr. Ray**, our baritone, a priest who's oh so dear

Now there's **Fr. Paul**, the youngest one, not wet behind the ears
He speaks Spanish fluently, serving Ecuador for years

Finally, we honor **Fr. Tevington** who's with the Lord above
Through his kindness and his gentle ways, he taught us how to love

So as we say goodbye to you in a sad and loving way
We extend our thanks and gratitude for your service day to day

Kevin McManus

Father, you are so gentle in your kindness and your grace
All your parishioners love you, and that glow upon your face
The first time that I met you, you made me feel at ease
Having an interest in your people, in all ways trying to please
Enlightened by the grace of God, you do your very best
Remembering the vows you took and all the many tests

Knowing you has gladdened me right from the very start
Everything you do with pride and loving from the heart
Very seldom do we meet a pastor with such zeal
Inspiring are your sermons that are quite sincere and real
Now serving at St. Pius V, your mission you'll fulfill
Fr. Kevin, we all thank you as you try to do God's will

Many sacrifices you have made in serving Christ the King
Caring with your cheerful smile and all the love you bring
My, how lucky I have been to know a priest like you
As always, you are there to help whenever skies are blue
Nothing in this world can make you lose your faith
Unending is your loyalty to God and to the human race
So, Father, thank you once again for all your caring ways
May God bless you forever, I pray for this each day

Blessed Trinity

Father, Son, and Holy Spirit, the **Blessed Trinity**
We believe this awesome mystery showing God's divinity
The ***Father's*** love is precious, and we know it to be true
He sent His only ***Son*** to earth to transform our souls anew
The ***Holy Spirit*** has a flame that ignites our very being
Three persons yet one God, one truth, through faith it is revealing
The Blessed Trinity, a special gift which comes from high above
Nurtures our souls throughout our lives, showing God's unending love

Jesus Christ, Our King

Jesus Christ died on Good Friday
To take away our sins
The son of the Almighty Father
Made heaven a place to win

He suffered on a cross of wood
A crown of thorns upon his head
In his agony, his sweat was blood
His tears for us he shed

On the third day, he arose
Glorious angels sang with joy
Heaven opened up its doors
And sin was then destroyed

Our Savior Jesus reigns on high
He's the king of all the earth
His passion, death, and resurrection
Was complete right from his birth

Let us give thanks to Christ our King
For all that he has done
Let us praise and honor him
For he is God's begotten Son

Thank you, my Lord and Savior
For forgiveness from above
I will worship you and praise you
You're my King, my God, my love

My Heart

My heart is a chapel where my Jesus lives
Without the Lord's graces, it's hard to forgive
My heart expresses deep emotions within
With my heart, I can love, I can hate, I can sin
My heart wants to share all the love Jesus gives
In my heart, I can feel that my Savior still lives
The heart of my Lord shines bright from above
I know in my heart, he has blessed me with love

Guardian Angel

Oh, guardian angel from above
Here once again beside me
To keep and watch each step I take
But most of all to guide me

When I am sad, you're by my side
To dry away my tears
Thank you so much for all your love
Now and throughout the years

Help me to serve my Lord and God
In everything I do
To love my neighbor as myself
And to all his laws be true

Please never let me see a soul
With malice or with greed
For we are all a part of God
And by his death, we're freed

So, guardian angel from above
Be with me all the way
Until I see the face of God
With your help, this I pray

May everyone upon the earth
Get closer to our Creator
For worldly things may come and go
But not the love of our dear Savior

Inner Search

There's a burning feeling deep within my soul
Sometimes I get the notion that I cannot reach my goals
For happiness seems far away, so far beyond my reach
I don't care to know the lessons others seem to want to preach

I've often tried hard to be understood
No one knows what I feel, or even if they could
This depressing emotion deep within my heart
Puzzles me at times for I know not where it starts

To ease this pain, it's hard for me
Sometimes my soul wants to be set free
To fly like a bird in boundaries beyond
In lands unknown or in silver ponds

I'm grateful for my faith in God
Which keeps me going with every trod
Searching for a brighter future, I gaze up at the sky
Without ever asking the famous question "Why?"

So don't give up or let life get you down
Just keep on smiling and hide all your frowns
For the time here on earth is very short
So live it to the fullest as a last resort

Shameful Ways

The soul cries out in horrid shame
Your behavior is unruly
You've made a nuisance of yourself
You should be embarrassed truly
A person does not act that way
So rowdy or so obnoxious
Fun can be expressed in many ways
That are not so quite atrocious
So think before you often act
And be proud for all your actions
So that others look at you with pride
And show a good reaction

Voice of the Soul

I feel an emptiness within and know not where it comes from
My soul seems to cry out in pain 'cause it wants to return home
This world is not a place for me with its hate and crime and lust
It's heaven where I want to be, with Jesus if I must

But my God, he has a plan for me, one that I must fulfill
Then I cannot go home with him until I do his will
So here I am oh so afraid and sometimes lonely too
God's the one who rules my life, and to him I shall be true

As I look to the horizon and see the sun appear
I know that better days will come because my Lord is near
So never let your burdens make you ever wear a frown
For if you trust in God above, he will never let you down

Lenten Time

A time to reflect on our transgressions
And become a better person in the future
A time to unite our minds and hearts to God
And prepare for the redemption of his Son
A time to not only experience the beauty of spring
But to feel the rejuvenation of the spirit
So what is the season of Lent?
A time to repent, a time to heal,
And a time to give praise to the Lord

At Times (A Reflection)

At times I feel as though life has treated me with such cruelty. And at times I have complained because many pleasures of life have been so very few to me. Then I recall the friends I've made along life's journey, and I realize that life has not been that cruel, for I have been blessed. So when I reflect on all of the bad experiences that I have had, I realize that much has also been given to me, such as wonderful friends, the gift of faith, and most of all the love of God.

Teacher Barbara—Bible Study

Bible teaching has been your gift to each and every one of us
Always so cheerful, so pleasant, as you give us all your trust
Regardless of how hectic your weekday may appear
Bringing us God's message is what your heart holds dear
At every Bible session, you bless us with your love
Reading scriptural passages given from our Lord above
Although we may not show it, you're close to all our hearts
Barbara, you are special, for God's knowledge you impart.

RCIA Team

Reaching out to our angel team who brings us faith and love
Christian teachings they impart with guidance from above
In all they do, they show they care, each lesson taught with zest
A blessing they are to all of us, and their knowledge we request
Time ends the waiting period; finally, our special day is here
Each prayer they said for all of us brought Christ to us so near
And now our journey's ended, and their support continues on
May we carry in our hearts each day the faith of God alone

Caring Physicians and Surgeons

Anatol Podolsky, MD

A first-class surgeon with hands of gold
Now with lots of pride, you're a man to behold
Always seeking to do what you think is right
To heal mankind with all your might
Operating is a skill, one you choose to do well
Lovingly, you do your job, your expertise dispel

Physician is your title, a professional for sure
Only you so willingly did bring about my cure
Diligently, you studied hard, a doctor you became
Orthopedics is your specialty, your name has such acclaim
Leading us and guiding us with advice and all your skills
Surely, your heritage denotes your dreams you did fulfill
Knowing you sets you apart from so many other healers
You're a figure skater, an athlete, a very high achiever

Joseph Mule, MD

Joseph, you're a surgeon with a gift from God above
Operating is your skill, which you do with such great love
Saving lives is your forte whenever there's a need
Every patient you treat special as you heal, they all agreed
Physician is your title, a professional for sure
Having you as my doctor was what brought about my cure

Many lives you have encountered in the years you've served mankind
Undoubtedly, you are quite special since you've always been so kind
Lovingly, you've helped us heal with advice and all your skills
Eternally, we are all grateful for we know you do God's will

Grace Young, MD

God made you a physician to heal all those in need
Reaching out with kindness has been your special deed
Acknowledging the hurts in life with love, you've done your best
Caring for others is your forte, you've done with such great zest
Every patient you treat special as you heal them with your skills

Your expertise delivered all your knowledge you instill
Only you so willingly serve mankind and God above
Undoubtedly, the kindness you have shown exhibit with great love
Not only have you shown to care, your thoughtfulness displayed
Grateful are the people who have trusted all your guiding ways

Precious Little Children

Our Precious Child

Suddenly, your child is born, an angel from above
One little beating heart projecting so much love
Five tiny fingers and tiny toes, so perfect as can be
I'm thrilled about our precious child, as you can surely see
A bundle of joy with cheeks so pink, God answered all our prayers
We love you very much, our sweet, and know we truly care
Each moment that we spend with you seems to brighten up our days
Loving you the way we do brings gladness in many ways
It seems that we are truly blessed when you came into our lives
Zealously, we watched you grow each day with such great pride
As we gaze at your angelic face and see your smile so sweet
We cherish all your lovely ways, they really can't be beat
Each day we are so thankful as we watch you play with grace
The years will pass and so will time, the memories we'll embrace
How lucky can two parents be seeing all your dreams come true
You brought us so much joy in life that no longer are skies blue

Danisito

Danisito is my angel, God's precious little boy
Always he is so playful that he fills my life with joy
Never a dull moment whenever he's around
In all his boyish gestures, he's just a little clown
Such a precious child to me as he kisses me each night
I pray that the Lord will bless him as I hug him very tight
Today he's just a little boy, tomorrow a grown a man
Oh, the memories I'll cherish as we walked along the sand

Gabriel

Gentle as a summer breeze your smile, oh, precious boy
Arriving early was God's plan to fill our hearts with joy
Brightened have been all our days right from the very start
Richly blessed our lives have been, you've captured all our hearts
In all creation, you came to us, a treasure from above
Each day, we're thankful to the Lord for our bundle of joy, our love
Lucky we've become to have a perfect child like you
Gabriel, when you were born, your parents' dreams came true

Michelle

My, what a beautiful baby girl everyone seems to say
In the month of October you were born, what a special day
Cuddly and so sweet, so precious as can be
Honey, you've brought lots of joy to everyone you see
Each time you come into our home, we love you more and more
Little angel of the Lord, your laughter we adore
Loving you was easy right from the very start
Every day we think of you 'cause you've captured all our hearts

Karyna

Karyna, my granddaughter, is such a joy to love
A precious little angel sent to me from God above
Recalling all my many prayers for a little girl to hold
Yes, finally you arrived, a treasure worth more than gold
Now my life is quite complete in oh so many ways
As I cuddle you in my arms, Karyna, each and every day

Zachary

Zooming here and running there, little baby in God's care
Always laughing, he's such a joy, my little darling baby boy
Cuddly to hold and so wonderful to love
How lucky am I with God's gift from above
Another precious life to call my very own
Rich as a treasure right here in my home
Yes, he is special and always will be
Zachary, my angel, is so precious to me

Christmas and New Year

Christmas

Christmas is a time for sharing
And giving from the heart
It's a time to think of those we love
Both near and far apart
It's opening up your heart with love
To everyone you meet
But most of all, it's that special time
To honor a babe so sweet
The gifts are just a gesture
Like the ones given to our King
But nothing can compare to the love
Which the Christmas season brings
Remember on this Christmas Day
That our Savior truly cares
And accepts you just the way you are
A child of God so fair

Christ's Special Birth

Upon a manger, a child did lay
On a very solemn Christmas Day
It was **Jesus** the son of **God**
So sweet and so divine
He came to save the world from sin
And bring peace to all mankind
Mary and **Joseph** were proud
And filled with so much love
They both felt blessed as chosen
Parents of this child from God above
The choirs of **angels** sang with joy
At the birth of this special baby boy
The **shepherds** in the fields were told
To go worship the **King of kings**
The **wise men** came to honor him
And very precious gifts did bring

Christmas King

Our King was born, sent from above
He wiped out hate and brought us love
On Christmas morn, the world got peace
Our Savior reigned, sin found defeat
The Magi worshipped, the shepherds came
A star shone bright, of Christ's birth proclaimed
All hearts were joyous, and souls found rest
For with Jesus's birth, the world was blessed
Christmas is the time of year, a gift to all mankind
May you and yours find love and peace and leave
your cares behind

A Christmas Prayer

Dear Lord, bless all my friends
This Christmas Day
Take all their cares and fears away
May they be given all good things
And all the joy that Jesus brings
May their hearts flourish in more love
For this I pray to God above
And may the New Year bring them peace
On this most holy blessed feast
Dear Lord, please bless my special friends
With peace on earth, good will toward men
I pray, dear Lord, with a pure heart
Thank you for friends both near and far

Christmas Tears

This Christmas Day, I cried a lot, and oh so many tears
A broken heart I got on this joyous day of the year
I felt so all alone and blue as though no one seemed to care
An emptiness just filled my soul, a feeling oh so rare
It seems as though I try to please and give love to everyone
Yet only heartache came my way, and all my joy was gone
No one deserves this sadness on such a special day
For all we really need is love to bring happiness our way

New Year

It's a year of new beginnings when the past is left behind
We envision a good future, the one who'll treat us kind
We ask for health and wealth and peace
For all good things that life can bring
We need to ask for greater faith to love the Lord our King
Let's forget about the past and look ahead to happier days
It's the New Year, time to change our many different ways
To get closer to the Lord and to love our fellow man
This very new beginning can bring peace throughout the land
Let this be the year to get all the good things you request
No matter what may lie ahead, always try to do your best
Happy New Year to you all, receive blessings from above
I wish you health and wealth and peace,
But most of all, God's love

Famous People

Ellen Degeneres

Each day, your show brings lots of joy and laughter
Loving your charisma, which will last forever after
Laughter is quite good for the soul, they seem to say
Ellen, with your smile, you brighten up our days
Nothing that we do in life is worth worrying about
For you help so many people, and that's without a doubt
During your show, viewing you makes us laugh with ease
Everything you say and do shows that you want to please
Generous and caring are all of your loving ways
Even on a gloomy day, your cheerfulness brings rays
Not allowing life's problems affect the way you feel
Each time your show comes on, your sincerity is real
Reaching out to others makes you special as can be
Enthusiastic as you dance, our problems are set free
So on this very special day, I wish you all the best
Ellen, it's your birthday, celebrate it with great zest

Oprah

Oprah, you're sensational in all your caring ways
People love you and your show that inspires us each day
Right from the very start, you were destined to shine bright
Although life did not treat you good, you fought back with all your might
How you have grown within yourself in spirit and in love
While the angels in the sky so high look proudly from above
In all the things you've said and done, you've shown others how to live
Never did you let your pain prevent your heart to give
From life experiences, you saw a need to make the world a better place
Reaching out to others everyday with such wit and with such grace
Even now, all the things you do bring us joy and lots of laughter
You are very special, Oprah, and will be remembered forever after

Painter of Light

The hues from your paintbrush light up God's creations
How they touch many hearts with such great revelations
Oh, what beauty is expressed in the brilliance of light
My, how gifted you are with your portraits so bright
As I gaze at the *Mountain Chapel* displayed on my wall
Such a feeling of calmness I feel deep within my soul
Kindling lights so inviting express all your love
In a world oh so dark, glorious realms shine above
No one has ever captured the warmth in your colorful paintings
Knowing and feeling God's love, you relay all his blessings
Always creating and expressing what you feel in your heart
Diligently, you add colors to canvas, biblical words you impart
Every portrait I see shows your talent expressed
Thomas Kinkade, you're special, and by God you've been blest

William W. Clinton—President

When did you think a great leader you'd be?
In the White House living and in the presidency
Longing to make America a better place to live
Leading us and guiding us with all you have to give
Immeasurable knowledge to us do you impart
America and its heritage, you hold dear within your heart
Many stipulations have often crossed your way

Joining other Democrats in decisions day to day
Enlightened by the grace of God, you do your very best
From the time you were elected, you experienced many tests
Future plans you have proposed to help your fellow man
Everything you do with pride for America your land
Running for election, you campaigned with all your might
Suddenly the US president, it sure was worth the fight
Once you were in office, you issued many bills
Never did you give up the fight, no one could destroy your will

Calmly you gave all your speeches and delivered them with pride
Letting all the people know that our country you would guide
In office for the first four years, you showed your compassionate ways
Now being reelected, we're really glad you stayed
Tomorrow brings the future with all its hope and dreams
Only with your great devotion you can make our rainbows beam
Now serving as our president again, your mission you'll fulfill
So who's our **forty-second** president? No other than you, Bill

Miscellaneous

America the Beautiful

America the beautiful, God's gracious gift to me
I came from Puerto Rico to a land of liberty

America the beautiful, a place where dreams come true
Where broken hearts are mended and saddened days are few

America the beautiful, the land that I adore
Throughout the years as I grew up good memories did endure

America the beautiful, with its majestic views
I've held you deep within my heart and my love for you just grew

America the beautiful, you've opened up your doors
May God's blessings be upon you in being a refuge to the poor

America the beautiful, always hold your children near
You've become a special part of me, you are so very dear

"Baby" (Millie's Kitten)

Baby, how I miss you to greet me day by day
Always you were there with me, and now you've gone away
I've shed so many tears for you 'cause I feel so all alone
I gave you all the love I could, and made my heart your home
You made me very happy throughout the many years
My precious little kitten, now I need to dry my tears

Broken Dreams

The world is full of broken dreams
And people with broken hearts
Yet God is with us at all times
Right from the very start

He chose us all to be his own
To do his holy will
And all along life's journey
The void in our hearts he fills

We need to know we're special
And not only in God's eyes
We need to love ourselves enough
And carry ourselves with pride

No matter what the world may think
Or what the people say
We've got to show them all our worth
And do our best each day

So please remember always
That everyone is loved
Don't let your feelings get you down
Just pray to God above

I know if you pray hard enough
And try to do your part
You'll overcome the struggles
That lie deep within your heart

Color My World

Color my world with rays of light
When darkness seems to rule
Color my world with laughter
When things seem to be cruel

Color my world with joy
When tears are all I know
Color my world with happiness
When sorrow seems to show

Once your world is colored
A rainbow oh so bright
You'll know that day is coming
And an ending to your night

Forgotten Souls

So fragile are those labored hands
Worn out from many years
So saddened are those lonely eyes
Which often fill with tears

Alone they sit, no one to care
Or even blink an eye
Who are all these forgotten souls
That seem to ask, "But why?"

Abandoned and so full of fear
Just aching for a touch
A little smile, a sweet hello
These treasures mean so much

So who are these forgotten souls
Who live with broken hearts?
You'll find them anywhere you look
On streets, in homes, in parks

Sadness

I feel an emptiness within
A sadness deep inside
My eyes keep filling up with tears
The pain I cannot hide
Why does it hurt so very much?
When trying to find joy
I go in all directions
My heart's a playful toy
My soul just wants to fly away
From this unending pain
My heart tells me to have more faith
For a new life will be gained

Graduation Day

Believe in all your dreams
And they will all come true
When things do not seem right
Have faith in all you do
Today is such a special time
It's your graduation day
Happiness will follow you
God will always guide your way

Margaret's Meat Loaf

Margaret got a meat loaf, the last piece of the bunch
She ate it very happily as her jaws chewed with a crunch
She thoroughly enjoyed it as others watched her eat
You would think she was performing a very special feat
The meat loaf got all eaten up until her plate was bare
Those who later wanted some thought it was totally unfair
For you see, she got the last piece at Carrows late that night
She really had a great time eating meat loaf made just right

God Will Pave the Way

A sadness has come over me, my spirit seems to cry
I cannot understand this pain that's burning deep inside
My eyes want to fill up with tears, yet something seems to say
Don't worry, all of this will pass for God will pave the way

I know life has its ups and downs, and pain will come and go
That time will heal the wounds and scars in my heart from long ago
Yet this emptiness still lingers on a void I cannot stand
I tell myself to have more faith and hold on to the Lord's hands

Young Ladies Institute (YLI)

YLI are special ladies who are mature yet young at heart
Our prayers and gifts to those in need, with love we do impart
Under Mary's great protection, she fulfills our every need
Now our caring is reflected in all our many deeds
God's grace is shed upon us for our generosity

Loyal to our Catholic faith as we serve humanity
Affection and respect, we share among the members of our clan
Diversity was very clear from the day our group began
Integrity, a principle that we all hold so dear
Encouragement to those we help, our values we adhere
Sisterly love, concern, and prayers are held in great esteem

Ideals are cherished every day as values that we deem
New members do uphold the virtues for which we stand
Sincerity, good will, and love, God's gifts to every man
Together we show charity to the less fortunate that we meet
Institute 188 is surely blessed with great endeavors at its feet
Trusting God's endearing love, our charity to all we share
Unending is our loyalty for our faith shows us to care
Tomorrows are still ahead as we continue to serve with love
Enjoying our institutional pledge to praise our God above

In Memoriam

In Loving Memory of Justina

Justina, you are special, chosen by God above
Upon your head, he placed a crown of everlasting love
Surely, you know God's angels are watching over you
The tears you shed are not in vain, for God knows your heart is true
In all you've done to share your love, you've made so many friends
Never will we forget your kindness, and all our love we send
Another year is almost gone, and many memories are shared
Justina, may God bless you, and please know how much we care

In Loving Memory of Stephanie

Suddenly I had to part and leave those that I love
The angel took my hand in his and showed me heaven above
Eternity is beautiful, with a sky so clear and blue
Perhaps I didn't realize God's promises so true
How sad I was to leave you the day God called my name
And when I saw my family there, my heart was not the same
Never had I seen such beauty, captivating and so grand
In green pastures now, I walk in the new and promised land
Eternal is my love for you, so please don't shed no tears
I'll be waiting here with open arms for you, my loving dears

Farewell to Velma

Velma, are you singing with the angels
From God's own heavenly home?
Are you smiling down from heaven
With that glow that's all your own?
You were always sweet and gentle
In your many caring ways
St. Pius Church won't be the same
Your greetings brightened up our days
We know that you are safely home
And in God's loving arms
Enjoying heaven and all its bliss
And now you're far away from harm
Yet we miss not having you around
To see your smiling face
Now that you have joined the angels
God has blessed you with his grace
Velma, please remember us
'Cause you'll live in all our hearts
Saying goodbye to you today
Brought sadness from the start
God bless you, our most loving friend
This is not a complete farewell
But just a very short goodbye
Until we meet again

A Tribute to Mapita (My Grandmother)

An angel sent from up above to teach me right from wrong
My grandmother stood by my side, a woman oh so strong
She loved me more than anyone could love me on this earth
And taught me the ideals of God and also my self-worth

The woman that I am today, I owe to my grandmother
She's in my heart and in my soul, like her there is no other
She taught me to always be kind and to myself be true
As she watched me growing up, her love for me just grew

Although I did not have a lot, I had the greatest treasure
An angel sent to me by God that really had no measure
This angel was Mapita, so loving and so kind
What made her very special was the fact that she was mine

The day the Lord took her from me, it truly broke my heart
For she was in my life so long I thought we'd never part
I know one thing my faith has taught, that we will be together
For life goes on beyond the grave to a land that's so much better

Mapita wears a crown of jewels, each gem for every hug and kiss
For all the kindness that she showed, the things that I now miss
It's really sad how some things change, how people come and go
Yet her love endures forever; her memory in my heart still grows

A Tribute to Milagros (My Mother)

Mother is the name you bear and are so deserving of
In all my growing years, you've given me your love
Lucky is the word I say to have a mom like you
As always, you are there to help whenever skies are blue
Gifted with such faith in God, you say your daily prayers
Recalling all your children, placing them in the Lord's care
Oh, mother, how I love you; you're so special to me
Sometimes I feel sadness because I'm far away from thee

May our hearts be reunited even though we're far apart
You are my pride and joy, dear Mom; I love you with all my heart

Milagros is the name that my dear mother bears
Only with such a heart of gold, she shows how much she cares
Tomorrow may never come, but for today I know
Her love is of the purest kind, and it always seems to grow
Everyone should have a mom as gentle and sweet as mine
Remembering her cheerful smile I shall treasure for all time

A Tribute to DiAngelo James Bono

During the eight years of your life, we were blessed with all your love
In our sorrow when you left, we knew you were called by God above
As time goes by, there isn't a day that you're not in our heart and mind
No one could've had a finer son, oh so loving and so kind
Gentle were all your ways even when you played your many games
Everything we wanted in a boy, we got the day you came
Loving you was such a pleasure 'cause you brightened up our days
Oh, if we have had more time to see more of your many ways

Joyous the occasion, the day you came to be
An angel that would fill our life with joy and ecstasy
Many moments come and go as we think back throughout the years
Each of us misses you so much and can't hold back the tears
So, little darling in the sky, we surely miss your laughter
James, you are our pride and joy for now and ever after

Beautiful memories that were made, we will cherish in our hearts
Oh, precious little child of ours, we knew it from the start
No one will ever take your place or our love for you so dear
Open up your tiny angel wings and hold us close and near

A Tribute to Jack Lore

Jack, you are so special to your dear ones and your friends
Always with your cheerful smile, sincere without pretense
Caring was a trait you had in your gentle ways and love
Knowing you was our great pleasure, a gift from God above

Lovingly, you touched the lives of your children oh so dear
Only with your heart of gold, you expressed your love so clear
Recalling all your years together, Joyce will treasure in her heart
Everlasting is your love and life that was there right from the start

A Tribute to Salvador

Suddenly you left us to go to the Lord above
Always cheerful in your ways and giving all your love
Lonely moments have been shared since you went away
Visually, your face appears, in our minds will always stay
Although you are not with us, our love still lingers on
Daddy, husband, loyal friend are names for you alone
One day we'll be together in such a heavenly place
Reminiscing of the life we shared as we gaze upon God's face

Deceased Children

Our children, whether small or grown
Are now gone to God's heavenly home
The angels came and held their hands
And led them to the promised land
With broken hearts, we watched them go
And one day we will meet, we know
Yet we are here, and they are there
In a land so beautiful and a sky so fair
Our sadness seems to consume us all
As we wait to hear God's gentle call
Your children are safe and happy with me
So don't be sad, they are all now free

About the Author

Joanne Concepcion Sanchez was born in Juncos, Puerto Rico, a small island in the Carribean. At the age of three, their mother moved them to America, and they settled in Philadelphia, Pennsylvania, where she was raised by her grandmother, since her mother was employed. Joanne had difficulty mastering the English language because only Spanish was spoken at home. Her mother then sent her to live with an aunt in Salt Lake City, Utah. There for one year, she was taught English by Missionary Mormons. When she returned to Philadelphia, she was speaking the English language fluently. Even though Joanne grew up in the East Falls housing project, throughout the years, she received a good education. In grade school at St. Bridget's, she was an honor student. In 1964, she graduated from John W. Hallahan Catholic Girls' High School. Later in life, she moved to Anaheim, California, and after being away from school for fourteen years, she returned, and in June 1982, she received an Associate's Degree in Human Services from Cypress College, and a Bachelor of Science Degree in June 1985 from California State University, Fullerton. Although her majors were in Human Services with a minor in Gerontology, the degrees that she obtained allowed her to get an employment working with an engineering firm in Westminster, California until she retired. Joanne truly believes that her God-given talent is a gift enabling her to express herself in her writings, especially through poetry.

CPSIA information can be obtained
at www.ICGtesting.com
Printed in the USA
FSHW010204040122
87370FS